AF394448

Focus

The focus of this book is:

- To follow a sequence of instructions,
- To look at the language of instructions.

 **Tuning In**

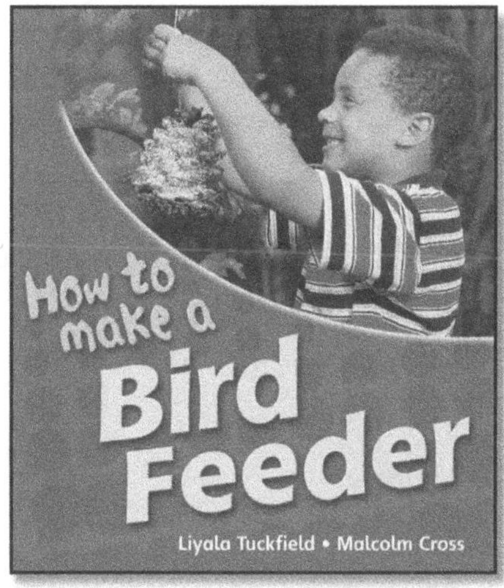

The front cover

Let's read the title together.

Why do we make bird feeders?

What birds do you think will come to the feeder?

How to make a Bird Feeder

Find out how to make a bird feeder from a pine cone and some peanut butter!

The back cover

What does the blurb tell us?

What would we need to make this bird feeder?

 **Tuning In**

Why do you think you need string and scissors?

 **Observe and Prompt**

Word Recognition

- If the children have difficulty with the words 'peanut', 'teaspoon' and 'birdseed', prompt them to break the words down into two syllables, before blending the whole words together.

- If the children have difficulty reading 'scissors', model the blending of this word for them. Explain the 'c' after the 's' is silent.

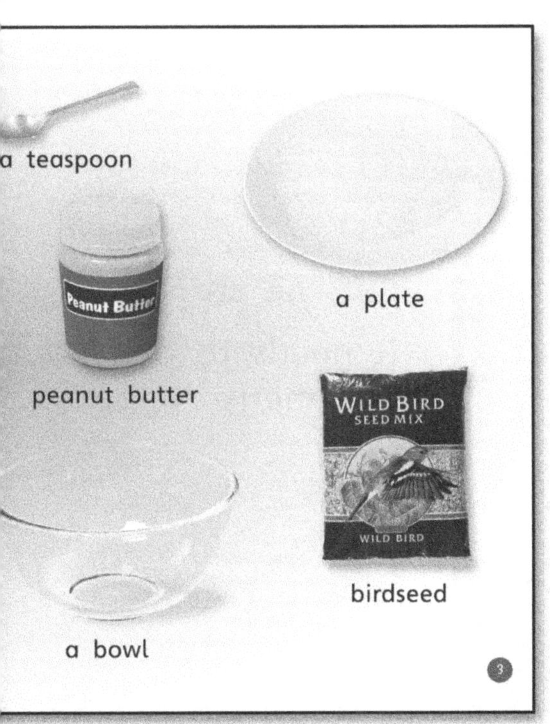

Observe and Prompt

Language Comprehension

- Ask the children what the labels show us.

- Check the children are able to identify the materials.

- Can the children think how these materials might be used to make a bird feeder?

 **Tuning In**

What do you think you do first?

 **Observe and Prompt**

Word Recognition

- If the children have difficulty reading 'metre', model the blending of this word for them.
- Help the children with the 'ou' sound in 'about' if they struggle with this word.

 **Step 1**

Cut the string.

It needs to be about one metre long.

4

 **Tuning In**

Why do you think you will need the string?

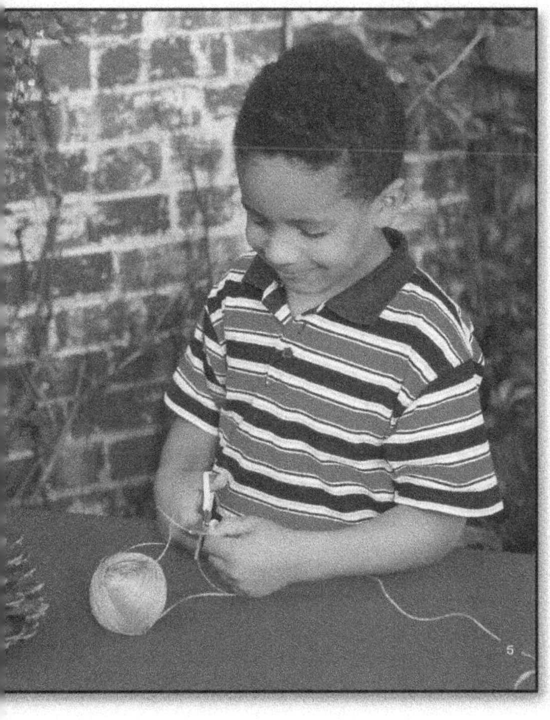

Observe and Prompt

Language Comprehension

- Check the children understand how long the string needs to be.
- What do the children think the boy will do with the string?
- Ask the children which step they think will come next.

5

 **Tuning In**

What is the boy tying the string to?

 **Observe and Prompt**

Word Recognition

- Check the children can read 'Tie' using their decoding skills.
- Check the children can read the vowel sounds in 'pine' and 'cone'.
- Check the children can read the sight words on this page 'to', 'the', 'of' and 'your' confidently.

 Step 2

Tie one end to the top of your pine cone

 Observe and Prompt

Language Comprehension

- Ask the children how they know this is the next step.

- Check the children understand that the instructions have to be followed in order.

- Ask the children what the boy is doing with the string.

 **Tuning In**

What do you think the boy is putting on the
pine cone?

 **Observe and Prompt**

Word Recognition

- If the children struggle to
  read 'peanut' and 'butter',
  prompt them to break
  these words down into
  two syllables, before
  blending the whole
  words together.

- Check the children can
  read 'your' with
  confidence.

 **Step 3**

Put peanut butter
on your pine cone.

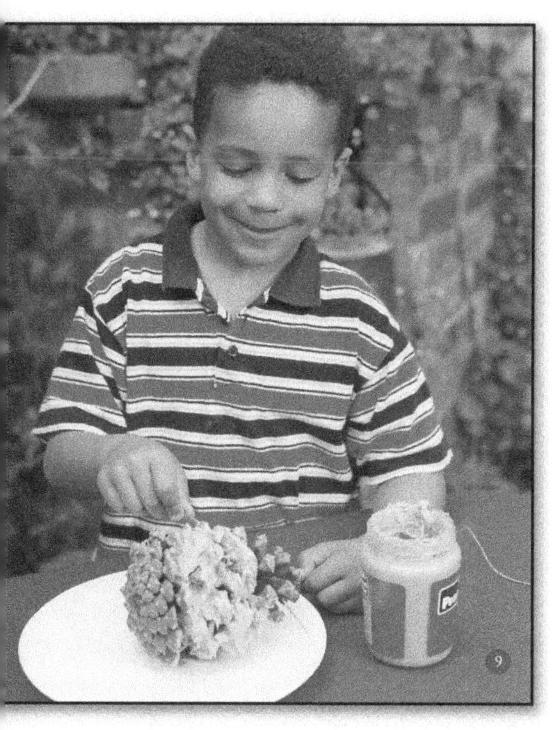

👁 Observe and Prompt

Language Comprehension

- Ask the children what the boy is using to put the peanut butter on the pine cone. Prompt them to look back to page 3 if necessary.

- Ask the children why they think the boy is putting peanut butter on the pine cone.

- Which step do the children think will come next?

Tuning In

Why do you think the boy is putting the birdseed in a bowl?

Observe and Prompt

Word Recognition

- Help the children with the 'ow' sound in 'bowl' if they struggle with this word.

- Prompt the children to break the word 'birdseed' down into two syllables, before blending the whole word together.

Step 4

Put the birdseed in a big bowl.

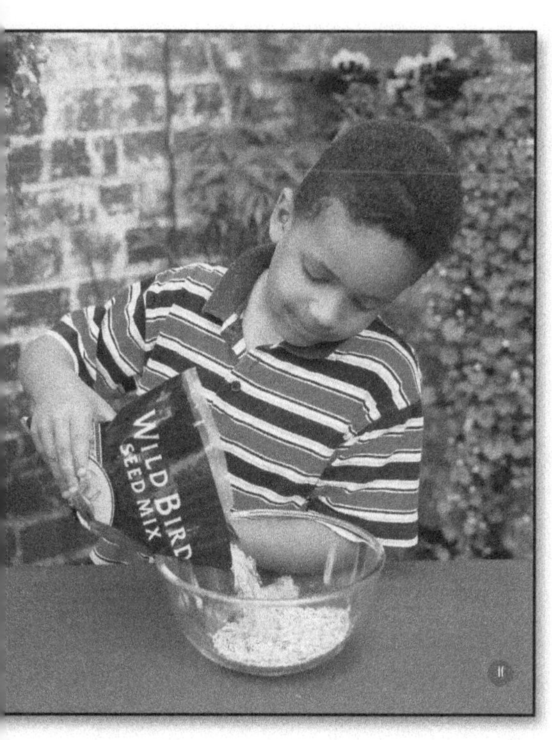

Observe and Prompt

Language Comprehension

- Ask the children which step this is.

- What do the children think the boy will do with the birdseed?

Tuning In

Why do you think the birdseed will stick to the pine cone?

 ## Observe and Prompt

Word Recognition

- If the children have difficulty reading 'Roll', model the reading of this word for them.

 **Step 5**

Roll your pine cone in the birdseed.

 **Observe and Prompt**

Language Comprehension

- Ask the children what the boy has to do in step 5.
- What do the children think he will do next?

Tuning In

What is the boy using to hang up his bird feeder?

Observe and Prompt

Word Recognition

- Help the children with the 'ow' sound in 'Now' if the children have difficulty with this word.

- If the children have difficulty reading 'ready', help them with the 'ea' sound in this word.

Step 6

Now your birdfeeder is ready.

Tie it to a tree.

Tuning In

What does he hope will happen now?

Observe and Prompt

Language Comprehension

- Ask the children what the boy is doing now.

- Do the children think birds will come to the birdfeeder?

 **Tuning In**

What are the birds doing?

 **Observe and Prompt**

Word Recognition

- Ask the children how this text is different.
- Do the children want to make this birdfeeder?
- Can the children remember what materials they need?